Seasonal Farmers Market Favorites

ALI KAPLON

ISBN: 1544675992
ISBN-13:9781544675992

ABOUT ALI

My passion for the culinary arts started when I was a child. I often experimented in the kitchen by creating concoctions with whatever ingredients and equipment I could find. I also loved helping my parents with dinner parties. It's always a joy to cook for people, make them happy and see the expression on their face.

I now run my personal chef business, Cooking Creations by Ali (alicooks.com) in Jacksonville, FL, give farmers market tours and teach a range of healthy cooking classes at Superior Body Sculpting. I've also taught for the University of North Florida's Osher Lifelong Learning Institute and at various synagogues.

To me, being involved with the culinary arts is a delight and an ongoing learning process that I will forever be happy to take part in.

CONTENTS

Introduction

Spring Recipes   1

Summer Recipes   16

Fall Recipes   50

Winter Recipes   72

MY BACKGROUND, THIS BOOK AND HOW YOU'LL BENEFIT

My love for food and cooking was cultivated at a young age. I have so many fond memories of family outings to pick fresh produce at nearby farms and having cookouts in the backyard with our fresh seasonal finds. As you can imagine, it was a pleasant experience to be surrounded by family and friends while eating tasty local food.

Being from Maryland, OLD BAY® Seasoning was always a constant in our cooking. Throughout this book, OLD BAY® finds its way into many of my favorite dishes. You might even notice some ingredients that reflect my heritage, which is Ashkenazi Jewish, with ancestors from Romania, Lithuania and Poland.

Today, I live in Jacksonville, FL. I have come to love this hidden treasure for its many fresh local foods. Because of the warm weather, there are great farmers markets almost year-round, with organic meats, cheeses and produce. You can also find all sorts of herbs and even baked goods. Here, there are two very popular local finds: Mayport shrimp and grouper. While your favorite local finds might differ, you are sure to stumble across some excellent regional delights.

As a personal chef and owner of Cooking Creations by Ali (alicooks.com), I incorporate ingredients from farmers markets in my clients' meals every day. It took some thought, but after being asked many times for recipes, I decided it was time to share some of them—and my love for the culinary arts—by writing this cookbook.

This book will inspire you to explore your local farmers markets to find fresh, organic foods. They will help keep you healthy and happy, and help local businesses and farmers thrive. As an added bonus, all of the recipes are not only flavorful, but also simple, so you will have plenty of time to live your busy life. With that said, let's start your journey towards cooking—and eating—some delicious, healthy meals with a local twist!

SPRING RECIPIES

Farmers Market Salad
Serves Six

Scrumptious Tips:
I have seen curly, dinosaur, Chinese and Red Russian kale at the farmers markets, but many other varieties exist. Kale is high in fiber, with each variety having a unique color and flavor ranging from mild to spicy, or even bitter. My favorite avocados are local Florida avocados, which are double the size of Hass avocados and have a light green color and a mild sweetness.

Salad Ingredients:
2 heads kale, center removed, chopped
1 pint grape tomatoes, sliced in half lengthwise
1 hot house cucumber, peeled and cubed
1 Florida avocado, pit and skin removed, cubed
1 4 oz container roasted pumpkin seeds

Vinaigrette Ingredients:
2 lemons, juiced
1/2 cup extra virgin olive oil
1 tsp Dijon mustard
1 tsp local honey
1/4 tsp sea salt
1/4 tsp black pepper

Salad Directions:
Mix ingredients together in bowl.

Vinaigrette Directions:
1. Whisk ingredients together until it thickens.
2. Add to salad.

Cucumber Salad
Serves Four

Scrumptious Tips:
Hot house cucumbers have a slightly sweet flavor and are perfectly bite-sized with a firm consistency, making them ideal for marinating in vinegar. To achieve a paper-thin slice for your cucumbers, try using a mandoline. I like to add fresh dill to this salad for an extra hint of flavor and color. This is a great make-ahead dish because it keeps well in the refrigerator for up to three days, while the flavors meld and intensify the longer it marinates.

Ingredients:
1 bottle seasoned garlic rice vinegar
1/4 tsp red pepper flakes
2 hot house cucumbers, peeled and sliced paper thin
1 bunch fresh dill, finely chopped

Directions:
1. Combine and stir together ingredients.
2. Marinate in refrigerator for minimum of 30 minutes, or overnight.
3. Use slotted spoon to remove cucumbers from liquid.

Lemon-Herb Honey Gold Potato Salad
Serves Six

Scrumptious Tips:
Honey gold potatoes have a natural buttery taste and texture. Olive oil binds the potatoes together, the same as mayonnaise, but is a lighter alternative with a different flavor profile. Substitute your favorite onion whether it's sweet, red, white or yellow, or a shallot or green onion for something different. This goes nice with another cold salad or your preferred fish or meat.

Ingredients:
2 lbs honey gold potatoes, skin on, cut in quarters
4 celery stalks, top and bottom removed, minced
1 sweet onion, skin removed, minced
1 fresh habanero pepper, seeds and pith removed, minced
1/2 bunch Italian flat leaf parsley, finely chopped
2 lemons, juiced and zested
1/4 cup extra virgin olive oil
1/4 tsp sea salt
1/4 tsp black pepper

Directions:
1. Cover potatoes with water in large pot and bring to boil. Cover and cook for 20 minutes. Drain and cool for 10 minutes.
2. Combine all ingredients until well incorporated.

Asian Style Cucumber Cups
Serves Eight

Scrumptious Tips:
Serve this dish inside cucumber cups as an appetizer, or omit the cucumber, and serve as a salad. You can bring a whole new life to the salad simply by adding your favorite shaped pasta, soy sauce alternative and/or different varieties of vinegar.

Ingredients:
4 cucumbers
8 oz gluten free rice spaghetti or whole wheat spaghetti
4 tbsp rice vinegar
3 tbsp reduced sodium soy sauce
2 tbsp sesame oil
3 green onions, sliced
1/2 package shredded carrots
1/2 tsp crushed red peppers

Directions:
1. Cook pasta according to cooking directions.
2. Drain and rinse noodles.
3. Peel cucumbers and slice into one-inch rounds. Scoop out middles.
4. Whisk together rice vinegar, soy sauce and sesame oil in small bowl. Add vegetables.
5. Add noodles to vegetable mixture and stir until well incorporated.
6. Scoop into cucumber cups.

Green Fruit Salad
Serves Four

Scrumptious Tips:
Originating in the Mediterranean, there are over 30 varieties of mint! Mint and lemon are a fantastic combination and give the salad a burst of light and refreshing flavor. Not to mention, lemons are high in vitamin C and great for your metabolism. Try experimenting with this recipe by using different fruit combinations each time you make it.

Ingredients:
2 cups green grapes, halved lengthwise
2 kiwis, peeled and chopped
1 honeydew melon, skin and seeds removed, chopped
1 lemon, juiced and zested
1 bunch fresh mint leaves, rolled up and thinly sliced

Directions:
In large bowl, combine and stir together all ingredients.

Fruit Sticks with Honey-Cinnamon Yogurt Dip
Serves Six

Scrumptious Tips:
Fruit sticks are suitable for all ages and can be served as a side dish with breakfast, lunch, dinner or dessert and as a snack. Try using your favorite fruits in different combinations each time you make them. My favorite honey is a local orange blossom variety, but use whichever variety you prefer. Make this dish a fun project with kids by cutting out fruit shapes with small cookie cutters.

Ingredients:
1 pineapple, cored, cut into chunks
1 cup green grapes, stem removed
1 cup red grapes, stem removed
1 pint strawberries, stem removed
1 16 oz container nonfat Greek yogurt
1 tsp cinnamon
1 tsp orange blossom honey

Directions:
1. Place fruits in alternating pattern on skewer stick.
2. In small bowl, whisk together yogurt, cinnamon and honey. Drizzle on top of each fruit stick or serve on the side as dip.

Star Fruit Salad
Serves Four

Scrumptious Tips:
Star fruit is a light green/yellow color and looks like a star when sliced crosswise. It's sweet and tastes like a cross between an apple and grape. To choose a ripe star fruit, look for a lighter color and softer texture while avoiding any that are too green or brown. The entire fruit can be consumed, including the seeds. Adding mint and lemon makes this salad crisp, light and refreshing.

Ingredients:
2 star fruit, thinly sliced crosswise
1 pineapple, cored and cubed
1 cup green Muscat grapes, halved lengthwise
1 package of mint, rolled and thinly sliced into chiffonade
1 lemon, zested and juiced

Directions:
Mix together and serve cold.

Broccoli Salad
Serves Four

Scrumptious Tips:

Be sure to use high quality vinegar that is naturally condensed and sweet—plain dark balsamic vinegar or one that is infused if you prefer. The broccoli adds a nice crunch to the salad, while the Greek yogurt adds a tanginess and creaminess, as well as additional protein. Always use organic cranberries, as they are naturally sweeter tasting. The salty sunflower seeds balance out the sweetness, allowing you to go sweeter or saltier.

Ingredients:

1 cup nonfat Greek yogurt
2 tbsp balsamic vinegar
1 head broccoli, chopped (florets and stems)
1/4 cup roasted and salted sunflower seeds
1 cup organic dried cranberries

Directions:

In large bowl, combine and stir together all ingredients.

Lemon Zest Cannelloni Bean Hummus
Serves Six

Scrumptious Tips:
Cannelloni beans are a softer texture than traditional garbanzo beans. Serve this dish with your favorite sliced vegetables or as a spread in a sandwich or wrap. Choose an organic lemon if you can, and use a fine microplane to zest it. When zesting, only use the yellow outside skin; the inner white pith is bitter.

Ingredients:
2 cans organic cannelloni beans, drained and rinsed
2 garlic cloves, skin removed
1 lemon, juiced and zested
1/4 tsp ground cayenne pepper
1 tsp ground cumin
1/8 tsp sea salt
1/8 tsp black pepper
2 garlic cloves, chopped
1/2 cup tahini paste
1/2 cup extra-virgin olive oil

Directions:
1. Combine all ingredients in food processor, excluding cayenne pepper and lemon zest, until it reaches a smooth consistency.
2. Sprinkle with cayenne pepper and lemon zest.
3. Serve with raw vegetables.

OLD BAY® Crab Deviled Eggs
Serves 12

Scrumptious Tips:

Incorporating crab meat adds a delicious twist to the traditional deviled egg. These can be served as an appetizer, on top of a salad or as a side item. Vegenaise® is a natural, healthy alternative to mayonnaise and can be found in the refrigerated section of your grocery store. OLD BAY® Seasoning, the traditional hometown favorite of mine, adds the perfect pop.

Ingredients:

12 eggs, hard boiled
1 8 oz container fresh crab meat
1/4 cup Vegenaise®
1/2 tsp OLD BAY® Seasoning
1 lemon, juiced
1 package chives, chopped

Directions:

1. Cover eggs with water and bring to boil. Then cover and turn off for 20 minutes before straining.
2. Peel, slice in half lengthwise, and scoop out yolk.
3. Whip all ingredients together, excluding egg whites, in food processor on high speed until it reaches smooth, filling-like texture.
4. Fill each egg white with filling using pastry bag with star tip.

Fruity Chicken Salad
Serves Four

Scrumptious Tips:
This works well on top of a bed of greens or as a sandwich with your favorite fresh bread. Be sure to purchase a firm, sweet apple and avoid those with a mealy texture. I like Pink Lady, Gala, Cameo, Empire, Fuji or Braeburn. If you prefer a finer textured chicken salad, try preparing it in a food processor. This dish can be made ahead of time and kept for up to three days in the refrigerator.

Ingredients:
4 cooked organic boneless skinless chicken breasts, chopped or pulled
1 cup nonfat Greek yogurt
1 cup red grapes, chopped
2 sweet red apples, chopped
1 bag dried cherries
1 lemon, juiced
1/2 cup toasted pecans
Dash of sea salt and pepper

Directions:
1. Combine all ingredients in food processor and pulse until well blended.
2. Serve on top of greens, as a sandwich or however else you like.

Waldorf Chicken Salad
Serves Six

Scrumptious Tips:
This is my take on the Waldorf salad, but with chicken instead of marshmallows. This salad packs a lot of flavor and great crunch! It can be made vegetarian simply by replacing the chicken with extra firm tofu. If you prefer a finer textured chicken salad, it can also be prepared in a food processor.

Ingredients:
4 cooked organic boneless skinless chicken breasts, chopped or pulled
2 cups nonfat Greek yogurt
2 cups red grapes, sliced in half lengthwise
2 sweet red apples, chopped
1/4 cup pecans, toasted and chopped
4 stalks celery, minced
Dash of sea salt and pepper

Directions:
1. In large bowl, combine and stir together all ingredients.
2. Serve on top of a bed of greens or as a sandwich with your favorite fresh bread.

Shrimp Mango Avocado Salad
Serves Four

Scrumptious Tips:
Mangoes are a tropical fruit with a sweet taste and soft texture. Avocados contain a generous amount of fiber, potassium, folic acid, good fat, and various vitamins and minerals, which help you feel full and satisfied. You will know when an avocado is ripe if it gives to the touch; avoid any with dark spots.

Ingredients:
1 and a 1/2 lbs small shrimp, peeled and deveined, cooked
1/2 cup 0% fat Greek yogurt
6 limes, juiced
2 mangoes, peeled and chopped
1 avocado, peeled and chopped
1 habanero pepper, stem, seeds and pith removed, chopped
1 bunch cilantro, chopped
Sea salt and black pepper to taste

Directions:
1. Bring one cup of water to boil, add shrimp and cook for two minutes or until it turns pink. Set aside.
2. In food processor, combine remaining ingredients and pulse until it reaches a chopped consistency.
3. In large bowl, stir together shrimp and yogurt mixture until well combined.
4. Serve on top of salad greens or inside wrap.

Sautéed Garlic Broccoli
Serves Four

Scrumptious Tips:
Broccoli contains lots of vitamins, fiber and antioxidants and can help with inflammation and aid in detoxification. Slightly charring broccoli gives the vegetable a whole new life when it comes to taste! Black sesame seeds add great color and crunch and are quite different than white sesame seeds. They can be found in the Asian section of your grocery store.

Ingredients:
1 tsp toasted sesame oil
3 cloves garlic, minced
1 head broccoli, cut into florets
1 tsp reduced sodium soy sauce
1/2 tsp black sesame seeds

Directions:
1. Sauté garlic and ginger in sesame oil on medium heat for one minute.
2. Add broccoli and cook for additional three minutes.
3. Drizzle with soy sauce and sprinkle with sesame seeds.

Turkey Burgers with Greek Yogurt Dill Sauce
Serves Four

Scrumptious Tips:
Turkey burgers are a fantastic weekly staple; there are many variations, making them a great go-to choice for lunch or dinner ideas. Grass-fed, lean ground beef or your preferred vegetarian crumble can be substituted for the ground turkey in this recipe. I like to serve them with grilled Cuban bread, or, for a low carb version, on top of salad greens topped with the yogurt sauce. This dip is great when you need a cool, refreshing snack on a warm day. This light, citrusy dip is delicious when scooped up with your favorite veggies, crackers or chips. You can even use it as the dressing in your tuna or chicken salads, or as a spread to add some zing to a sandwich! A bonus? It can be stored in the refrigerator for up to three days.

Burger Ingredients:
1 lb 97% fat-free, organic ground turkey
1/4 cup Worcestershire sauce or alternative
A dash of salt and black pepper
1 tsp Italian seasoning
1 organic egg
1/3 cup panko bread crumbs

Sauce Ingredients:
1 container 0% fat Greek Yogurt
1 lemon, juiced
1 tsp minced garlic
1 small bunch fresh dill

Burger Directions:
1. Mix ingredients listed for burgers together by hand.
2. Form into four patties.
3. Grill on high heat for six minutes on each side, or until it reaches an internal temperature of 165° F and is no longer pink. Another alternative is to bake at 350° F for 30 minutes on a greased, nonstick foil-lined baking sheet.

Sauce Directions:

1. Mix together yogurt, garlic, lemon and dill.
2. Serve as open-faced sandwich on your favorite bread or bun, or on top of a bed of fresh greens topped with a dollop of sauce.

Pineapple Rice
Serves Six

Scrumptious Tips:

Pineapple has a vibrant flavor that matches its color; it tastes tart and sweet at the same time, with a tender texture. Short grain brown rice sticks together nicely and is the best variety of rice for this dish. Coconut oil is great to cook with because it has a high smoke point (when the oil is added to the pan, breaks down and smokes) of 350 F.

Ingredients:

1 tsp organic coconut oil
Sea salt and black pepper to taste
1 cup short grain brown rice
2 cups organic vegetable broth
1/4 cup seasoned rice vinegar
1 bunch scallions, thinly sliced
1/2 red chili pepper with stems, seeds and pith removed, minced
1 pineapple, skin and core removed, finely chopped

Directions:

1. Cook rice according to package directions, replacing water with vegetable broth.
2. Stir rice vinegar into hot rice and set aside.
3. Sauté additional ingredients with coconut oil on medium-high heat for five minutes, or until lightly browned.
4. Stir together rice and pineapple mixture.

SUMMER RECIPIES

Shrimp Salsa
Serves Six

Scrumptious Tips:
Making this dish ahead of time saves you time preparing dinner later and allows the flavors to fully meld and come alive. It can remain in the refrigerator for up to three days. Serve on top of your favorite protein such as fish or chicken, on top of greens, or with your favorite tortilla chips. If you prefer a vegan version, substitute your favorite vegan protein such as Beyond Meat, tofu or tempeh.

Ingredients:
1 lb fresh jumbo shrimp, cleaned
1 pint grape tomatoes
1 red onion, top and tail removed, rough chopped
1 jalapeño pepper, stemmed, seeds and pith removed
4 limes, juiced
1 bunch cilantro
1/4 tsp salt

Directions:
1. Cover shrimp with water, bring to boil, cook for two minutes until shrimp turns pink, and drain.
2. Put shrimp and additional ingredients into food processor and pulse until it reaches a chunky consistency.

Grilled Stone Fruit over Greens
Serves Four

Scrumptious Tips:
Examples of stone fruit are plums, peaches, nectarines, cherries and mangoes. They have a small pit inside, also called a drupelet, meaning "little drupe." Cooking on the grill brings out the natural caramelization and sweetness of the fruit.

Ingredients:
1/4 cup strawberry flavored balsamic vinegar from the Olive Oil Store
1/3 cup extra virgin olive oil
1 tbsp Dijon mustard
1 tsp honey
2 peaches, pitted and sliced
2 nectarines, pitted and sliced
2 apricots, pitted and sliced
4 plums, pitted and sliced
1 small package goat cheese, crumbled
1/4 cup toasted almonds
1 large container baby greens

Directions:
1. Grill fruit on high heat for two minutes on each side, then set aside.
2. Whisk together vinegar, oil, mustard and honey until it thickens, then set aside.
3. Assemble salad together, and top with goat cheese, almonds and vinaigrette.

Berry - Kale Salad
Serves Four

Scrumptious Tips:
One of the best superfoods available, dark green leafy kale is packed full of calcium and other vital nutrients. There are many varieties of kale, but I prefer the black, flat-leaf version for this salad. For the dressing, choose a cold-pressed, extra virgin olive oil. Cold-pressed olive oil is made by pressing ripe olives without the use of chemicals or heat, leaving you with the highest quality and best tasting olive oil.

Salad Ingredients:
1 bunch black, flat-leaf kale, ribs removed and chopped into bite-sized pieces
1 package strawberries, greens removed and sliced
1 package blackberries
1 package blueberries
1 banana, sliced
1 package mint, stem removed and thinly sliced

Dressing Ingredients:
1/4 cup strawberry balsamic vinegar
1/4 cup cold-pressed extra virgin olive oil
1 tsp local honey
1 tsp Dijon mustard

Directions:
1. Toss all ingredients together to assemble salad.
2. Whisk together vinegar, oil, honey and Dijon to make dressing and drizzle on top.

Heirloom Tomato Salad
Serves Four

Scrumptious Tips:
This is a great farmers market salad. Try organic tomato varieties, as they have sweeter and more robust flavor and help you avoid unwanted chemicals in your diet. Using fresh chives will provide more taste than dried chives. I love to use fresh herbs whenever they are available, and growing your own is even better!

Salad Ingredients:
4 heirloom tomatoes, thinly sliced
2 carrots, shaved

Dressing Ingredients:
1/4 cup white wine vinegar
1/4 cup cold-pressed extra virgin olive oil
1 package fresh chives, thinly sliced
1 lemon, juiced
2 garlic cloves, minced
1 tsp local honey
1 tsp Dijon mustard

Directions:
1. Arrange tomatoes and carrots in layer on platter.
2. In separate bowl, whisk together ingredients for dressing.
3. Drizzle dressing on top of salad.

Tabbouleh Salad
Serves Four

Scrumptious Tips:
Tabbouleh salad is a light and colorful Mediterranean dish that is packed with lots of healthy herbs and vegetables. I love to use Za'atar spice blend, which can be purchased either in-store or online at penzeys.com, in this salad. This dish can be prepared and kept in the refrigerator up to three days.

Ingredients:
1 and 1/2 cups uncooked bulgur wheat
1 bunch flat leaf parsley, chopped
1 bunch fresh mint, chopped
2 hot house cucumbers, peeled and chopped
1 pint organic grape tomatoes, cut in half lengthwise
1/4 cup green onions, chopped
2 Meyer lemons, juiced
1 tbsp extra virgin olive oil
A dash of sea salt and black pepper
1/2 tsp Za'atar spice blend
1/2 tsp sumac

Directions:
1. Follow cooking directions on back of box for bulgur wheat.
2. Add ingredients and stir together.
3. Serve cold.

Fattoush Salad
Serves Four

Scrumptious Tips:
Fattoush salad consists of Mediterranean seasonal vegetables such as tomatoes, cucumbers, parsley and mint. The dressing contains lemon juice, olive oil and sumac, a tangy and peppery spice that can be found in stores or online from Penzeys Spices.

Salad Ingredients:
2 large pieces whole-wheat pita bread, cut into wedges
1 tbsp olive oil
3 heads (one package) organic romaine lettuce, chopped
1 bag shredded cabbage
1/2 cup fresh mint, chopped
1/2 cup fresh Italian parsley, chopped
2 scallions, chopped
1 pint grape tomatoes, halved lengthwise
1 hot house cucumber, peeled and chopped

Dressing Ingredients:
2 lemons, juiced
1 tbsp white wine vinegar
1 tsp Dijon mustard
1/3 cup cold-pressed extra virgin olive oil
1 tbsp local honey
1/2 tsp sumac powder
2 tbsps fresh mint, stems removed
A dash of sea salt and black pepper

Salad Directions:
1. Preheat oven to 375° F and line baking sheet with nonstick foil.
2. Cut pita into eight wedges, arrange in single layer on baking sheet, drizzle with oil, and bake for 12 minutes (turning every four minutes).
3. Assemble salad together, topping with pita crisps.

Dressing Directions:
Pulse in blender or food processor until it reaches a smooth consistency.

Tomato Cucumber Relish
Serves Eight

Scrumptious Tips:

This relish is a great complement to any dish that you want to give an additional punch of flavor and color. Tomato cucumber relish adds wonderful, fitting flavors to the Middle Eastern Spiced Chicken recipe in this book.

Ingredients:

1 hot house cucumber, peeled and roughly chopped
1 sweet onion, roughly chopped
1 pint grape tomatoes, chopped
1 clove garlic, peeled and roughly chopped
1 lemon, juiced
1 tsp red wine vinegar
1 bunch flat leaf parsley, chopped
Dash of sea salt and black pepper

Directions:

Combine all ingredients in food processor and pulse until finely chopped. Use to top your favorite meat or seafood dish.

Watermelon Gazpacho
Serves Four

Scrumptious Tips:
Gazpacho is made of raw fruits and vegetables, pureed and served cold. There are many variations of gazpacho, making it a no-fail recipe. Feel free to fit your preferences and replace the peppers with your favorite pepper and the juices with your favorite juice to add a personal twist. The yogurt and mint add a refreshing and creamy touch!

Ingredients:
1 large watermelon, rind removed, rough chopped
1 seedless cucumber, peeled
1/2 jalapeño pepper, seeds and pith removed
1/2 habanero pepper, seeds and pith removed
1 red pepper, seeds and pith removed, rough chopped
3 cloves garlic
1 red onion, skin removed, rough chopped
1 bunch parsley, rinsed, stems removed
2 limes, juiced
1 naval orange, juiced
1 small container 2% FAGE Greek yogurt
1 bunch mint, rolled, thinly sliced

Directions:
1. In blender, puree all ingredients, excluding mint and yogurt, until smooth.
2. Pour into bowls and top with dollop of yogurt and sprinkle of mint.

Roasted Tomato Medley
Serves Four

Scrumptious Tips:
Shop at your nearby farmers market for fresh organic tomatoes. Considered a fruit, tomatoes come in many varieties including cherry, beefsteak and heirloom. Chiffonade the basil by rolling it up and thinly slicing through it so it looks like ribbons. It makes a beautiful and colorful presentation! You can either make your own balsamic reduction by simmering over medium heat until reduced, or you can purchase my favorite dark balsamic reduction from the Olive Oil Store.

Ingredients:
6 cloves garlic, peeled and minced
1/4 cup olive oil
1/4 tsp smoked sea salt
1/4 tsp cracked pepper medley blend (pink, red, black pepper mix)
2 packages yellow grape tomatoes
2 packages red grape tomatoes
3 sprigs fresh oregano, sprigs removed
1/8 cup dark balsamic vinegar reduction
1 package fresh basil, stems removed, chiffonade

Directions:
1. Preheat oven to 450° F.
2. Line baking sheet with nonstick foil.
3. Toss all ingredients together, excluding basil.
4. Spread tomato mixture in single layer on baking sheet.
5. Place tomatoes and olive oil on nonstick foil on baking sheet in single layer and roast at 450° F for 24 minutes, then broil on high heat for one minute.
6. Remove from oven, drizzle with dark balsamic vinegar, and sprinkle with basil chiffonade.

Tomato, Basil and Mozzarella Sticks with Balsamic Glaze
Serves Eight

Scrumptious Tips:
With fresh tomatoes and basil at their peak during summer, it makes sense to put them together for a fresh, light and delicious appetizer or snack. These are easy to put together and make for a fun, portable snack. You can find my favorite Cherry Balsamic Glaze at The Olive Oil Store, but any balsamic glaze can be substituted.

Ingredients:
1 package small skewer sticks
1 package grape tomatoes, rinsed and dried
1 package basil, picked from stem
4 containers baby fresh mozzarella balls
Dash of sea salt and black pepper
Drizzle of cherry balsamic glaze

Directions:
Place a grape tomato, ball of basil and mozzarella square on each skewer, then add salt, pepper and balsamic glaze. Repeat process.

Sun Butter Shrimp and Ginger Stir-Fry
Serves Four

Scrumptious Tips:
Here in Jacksonville, FL, we are lucky to have a local source of fresh-caught shrimp available from nearby Mayport. Any kind of shrimp will do, but I always urge to buy local if you have access. Sun butter is a great alternative to peanut butter for those who have a peanut allergy. If you do not care for the taste of sun butter and have no problem with peanuts, use creamy organic peanut butter.

Ingredients:
1 lb jumbo shrimp, peeled and deveined
Sea salt and black pepper to taste
1 lime, juiced and zested
1 tbsp reduced sodium gluten free soy sauce, Bragg Liquid Aminos or coconut aminos
1/2 tsp fish sauce
1/2 tsp sesame oil
1/8 tsp red pepper flakes
1/2 tsp black sesame seeds
2 cloves garlic, minced
1 inch fresh ginger, grated
2 limes, juiced and zested
1 tsp seasoned rice vinegar
1 tbsp creamy sun butter
1 package baby bella mushrooms, chopped
1 yellow squash, top and tail removed and chopped
1 zucchini, top and tail removed and chopped
1 package shredded carrots
6 sweet baby bell peppers, pith and seeds removed, thinly sliced
1/4 cup sunflower seeds
1 bunch scallions, thinly sliced
1 bunch cilantro, stems removed, finely chopped
1 cup cooked brown rice

Directions:
1. Sauté shrimp in small amount of sesame oil on medium-high heat for three minutes, then set aside.

2. Stir together all additional liquid ingredients and spices in small bowl, then set aside.

3. Turn heat up to high, add all ingredients except for sunflower seeds, scallions, cilantro and rice, and bring to boil (allowing it to thicken).

4. Turn down to simmer and stir in shrimp.

5. Garnish with sunflower seeds, scallions and cilantro.

6. Serve with brown rice.

Honey Mustard Salmon
Serves Four

Scrumptious Tips:
For the best flavor and healthiest choice, choose a fine, organic Dijon mustard and local raw honey. Any variety of local honey will work, but my favorite here in Florida is orange blossom honey. Give this dish a nice pop of color and flavor by garnishing with fresh herbs. This is healthy, delicious and easy to throw together, making it perfect for a busy weeknight meal.

Ingredients:
4 pieces of 8 oz salmon, skin on
2 large lemons, juiced
1/4 cup organic Dijon mustard
1/8 cup local honey
1 poblano pepper, stem, seeds and pith removed, finely chopped
1 tsp minced garlic
1 bunch dill, finely chopped
1 bunch chives, thinly sliced
1 bunch cilantro, stems removed, finely chopped

Directions:
1. Preheat oven to 350° F.
2. Line baking sheet with nonstick foil.
3. Spread fish in single layer.
4. Use fork to poke holes in fish.
5. Sprinkle with all ingredients, excluding chives and cilantro, adding honey last.
6. Bake for 14 minutes, then broil for one minute on high heat.
7. Remove skin with spatula.
8. Garnish with chives and cilantro.

Dijon Roasted Chicken with Local Fruit Preserves
Serves Four

Scrumptious Tips:
Chicken thighs are great for make-ahead meals as bone-in dark meat retains more moisture when reheated. Other preserves, such as raspberry, strawberry or peach may be substituted for apricot preserves, but finding fresh, locally made preserves is best. If you have no local options, choose a brand that uses the least amount of ingredients and preservatives. Chicken is cooked through once it reaches 165° F, so if you are unsure, place a meat thermometer into the thickest part of the chicken to get an accurate reading. Allow the meat to rest for 1/3 of its cooking time to allow the juices to seal in.

Ingredients:
8 organic bone-in chicken thighs, skin removed
1/4 cup Worcestershire sauce
Dash of sea salt and black pepper
4 garlic cloves, minced
4 tbsp Dijon mustard
4 tbsp local, organic fruit preserves
1 bunch green onions, finely chopped

Directions:
1. Preheat oven to 375° F.
2. Line baking sheet with nonstick foil and spray with oil.
3. Marinate chicken in Worcestershire sauce for 30 minutes.
4. Sprinkle chicken with dash of salt and pepper.
5. Microwave Dijon mustard and fruit preserves on high power for 45 seconds, stir, and then cook for additional 30 seconds.
6. Brush mixture on top of chicken.
7. Roast for 49 minutes, then broil for one minute.
8. Sprinkle with green onions

Grilled Chicken with Pineapple Salsa
Serves Four

Scrumptious Tips:
This simple, light and satisfying dish is perfect for a summer barbecue with friends and family. Any extras keep well in the refrigerator for up to three days and are delicious when thinly sliced across the grain and served cold or hot on top of a salad, in a sandwich or in a wrap. Great for make-ahead meal planning for busy weekdays!

Ingredients:
1 lb thinly sliced chicken breast
1/4 cup Worcestershire sauce
1 lemon, juiced
1 tsp Tex-Mex spice blend
1/2 pineapple, finely chopped
1 jalapeño (seeds removed), minced
1 red pepper (seeds removed), minced

Directions:
1. Marinate chicken in Worcestershire sauce, lemon and Tex-Mex spice blend for at least 30 minutes.
2. Grill chicken on medium-high heat for 4-5 minutes on each side, then set aside.
3. Combine remaining ingredients and stir together.
4. Top chicken with salsa.

Chicken Satay with Coconut Peanut Dipping Sauce
Serves Four

Scrumptious Tips:
While this dish is great for lunch or dinner, try serving it at your next get-together for a delightful, easy-to-eat party food that will please any crowd.

Chicken Ingredients:
2 packages chicken tenderloins
2 limes, juiced
1/4 cup soy sauce or soy sauce alternative
1 tsp crushed red pepper
Dash of garlic salt, black pepper and paprika
1 package medium skewer sticks

Sauce Ingredients:
1 can unsweetened coconut milk
1/4 cup peanut butter
1 tbsp honey
1 lime, juiced

Chicken Directions:
1. Marinate chicken in lime juice, soy sauce and crushed red pepper for at least 10 minutes.
2. Remove from marinade, and sprinkle with garlic salt, black pepper and paprika.
3. Grill on high heat for three minutes on each side.
4. Remove from heat and vent with foil.

Sauce Directions:
1. Whisk together coconut milk, peanut butter, honey and lime juice on medium heat until it reaches a boil. Then, turn down to low heat and whisk constantly for two minutes.
2. Serve chicken with dipping sauce.

Island Cilantro-Garlic-Lime Shrimp
Serves Four

Scrumptious Tips:
If fresh red chili peppers are unavailable, you can replace with 1/4 tsp crushed red pepper flakes. Use fresh jumbo shrimp, as they have a sweeter and more succulent flavor. This dish can be made vegan by replacing the shrimp with tofu.

Ingredients:
1 tbsp coconut oil
4 garlic cloves, skin removed, minced
2 lbs fresh jumbo shrimp, cleaned
4 limes, juiced and zested
1/2 fresh red chili pepper, stem, seeds and pith removed, minced
Sea salt and black pepper to taste
1 bunch cilantro, stems removed, minced

Directions:
1. Heat skillet on medium-high heat with coconut oil.
2. Add garlic and shrimp and sauté for two minutes.
3. Add lime juice and cook for an additional one minute.
4. Add sea salt and black pepper.
5. Garnish with cilantro.

Chili-Lime Chicken with Tahini-Yogurt Sauce
Serves Six

Scrumptious Tips:

Citrus zest adds a nice zing. Use a fine microplane and make sure you only remove the outer skin, as the white pith underneath is bitter. The sauce is made with tahini, which is a paste made from ground sesame seeds. This dish is versatile and can also be prepared with your favorite seafood or tofu.

Chili-Lime Chicken Ingredients:

6 organic chicken breast cutlets, pounded out and poked with fork on both sides
4 limes, juiced and zested
2 tbsp olive oil
1 tbsp chili powder
1 tbsp cumin
1 bunch green onions, top and tail removed
4 garlic cloves, skin removed
1 bunch cilantro
Sea salt and black pepper to taste

Tahini-Yogurt Sauce Ingredients:

1 five oz container nonfat Greek yogurt
1 tbsp tahini paste
1 lime, juiced
Sea salt and black pepper to taste

Chili-Lime Chicken Directions:

1. Combine all ingredients, excluding chicken, in food processor and pulse until smooth.
2. Cover chicken with marinade and place in glass food storage container, covered in refrigerator for at least 20 minutes.
3. Heat grill to medium-high.
4. Remove chicken from marinade and grill chicken for five minutes on each side, or until it reaches 165° F inside.
5. Allow chicken to rest for three minutes.
6. Thinly slice chicken.

Tahini-Yogurt Sauce Directions:
1. Whisk together tahini yogurt sauce ingredients until well combined and smooth.
2. Serve cold poured on top of chicken or on side.

Citrus-Rosemary Roasted Chicken
Serves Four

Scrumptious Tips:

This recipe is easy to throw together, yet an exciting way to jazz up roasted chicken with fresh rosemary and lemon zest. When marinating, poke the chicken on the front and back with a fork to allow the marinade to infuse into the chicken for the best flavor.

Ingredients:

8 organic chicken thighs, skin removed
1/4 cup Worcestershire sauce
4 garlic cloves, minced
Salt and pepper to taste
1/4 tsp ground cayenne pepper
1 lemon, juiced and zested
4 sprigs fresh rosemary

Directions:

1. Marinate chicken in Worcestershire sauce for at least 30 minutes.
2. Preheat oven to 375° F.
3. Line baking sheet with nonstick foil and spray with oil.
4. Sprinkle marinated chicken with salt and pepper.
5. Add lemon juice, zest, cayenne pepper and rosemary.
6. Roast for 49 minutes, then broil for one minute.

Sweet and Sour Pineapple Chicken
Serves Four

Scrumptious Tips:
This is a lighter alternative to the sweet and sour chicken you would normally order from a Chinese restaurant. Be sure to use fresh pineapple, not canned. Adjust the spice level to fit your preference. If you prefer yours extra spicy, substitute 1/2 fresh minced red chili pepper for the red pepper flakes. You will know the chicken is cooked through once the internal temperature reaches 165° F.

Ingredients:
4 cooked organic boneless skinless chicken breasts, cut to bite sized pieces
6 oz jar of good quality apricot jam
1/4 cup reduced sodium soy sauce
1/4 cup rice vinegar
1 fresh pineapple, cored and cubed
1 bunch scallions, thinly sliced
1/2 fresh red chili pepper, stem, seeds and pith removed, minced, or 1/4 tsp red pepper flakes
Salt and pepper to taste
1 bunch fresh cilantro, stems removed and finely chopped
1 tbsp black sesame seeds

Directions:
1. In large bowl, combine all ingredients, excluding cilantro and sesame seeds.
2. Heat up large nonstick skillet on high heat, add ingredients, bring to boil, and stir. Reduce heat to simmer, cook uncovered for eight minutes, or until sauce has thickened and chicken is cooked through.
3. Garnish with cilantro and black sesame seeds.

Sweet and Sour Meatballs
Serves Four

Scrumptious Tips:

This dish can be made using either ground turkey or ground beef. To avoid dry meatballs, do not use all white meat or fat free ground turkey. 94% fat free ground turkey is my usual go-to. Traditional meatballs with tomato sauce or gravy are definitely delicious, but this is the perfect way to try something different and exciting.

Meatball Ingredients:

1 lb ground turkey (94% fat free)
1/2 bunch scallion, minced in food processor
1/2 cup whole wheat or gluten free breadcrumbs
1 egg
Salt and pepper to taste

Sweet and Sour Sauce Ingredients:

2 small jars of good quality apricot jam
1/4 cup reduced sodium soy sauce
1/4 tsp fresh red chili pepper, stem, seeds and pith removed, minced, or a dash of crushed red peppers

Meatball Directions:

1. Preheat oven to 350° F.
2. Line baking sheet with nonstick foil and rub with olive oil.
3. Roll into walnut sized balls, space out evenly in a single layer on the baking sheet, and cook for 30 minutes.

Sweet and Sour Sauce Directions:

1. Combine ingredients in small to medium sized saucepan.
2. Bring to boil over medium-high heat.
3. Reduce heat to low and simmer for three minutes.
4. Pour over meatballs or serve alongside meatballs for dipping.

Asian Style Chicken Lettuce Wrap
Serves Four

Scrumptious Tips:
This dish is delightfully colorful, fresh and delicious! I prefer to use brown rice to add more substance, but if you are watching your carbs, the rice can be omitted. The butter lettuce has a light flavor and adds a nice crunch to the wrap. This can be converted to a salad by pulling the lettuce leaves apart, layering them on a plate and placing the filling on top. Look for black sesame seeds in the ethnic food section of your grocery store.

Ingredients:
1 tsp coconut or sesame oil
1 lb ground chicken, 60% fat free
1 can diced water chestnuts, rinsed and drained
2 garlic cloves, minced
2 inch piece ginger, grated
1 package sugar snap peas, chopped
1 package mushrooms, chopped
1 cup shredded carrots
2 tbsp reduced sodium soy sauce
1 tsp local honey
1 bunch scallions, thinly sliced
1 tsp black sesame seeds
2 heads butter lettuce, separated
1 1/2 cups cooked brown rice

Directions:
1. Sauté chicken, scallions, garlic and ginger in coconut oil on medium-high heat until chicken is cooked through and no longer pink (about two minutes).
2. Add vegetables and cook for additional two minutes.
3. Stir in rice.
4. Wrap mixture inside lettuce leaf.

Asian Skirt Steak with Grilled Balsamic Pineapple
Serves Four

Scrumptious Tips:
Choose outside cuts of skirt steak, as they are naturally tenderer than inner cuts. Since this is such a thin cut of meat, it will cook quickly, so be careful. After grilling, thinly slice against the grain to seal in the juices and preserve the texture.

Ingredients:
2 lbs outside skirt steak
1/4 cup Worcestershire sauce
1/2 cup reduced sodium soy sauce
1 inch ginger, peeled and grated
4 garlic cloves, peeled and minced
Black pepper to taste
2 pineapples, core removed
1 tbsp balsamic glaze

Directions:
1. Marinate steak in Worcestershire sauce, soy sauce and black pepper for at least 30 minutes.
2. Remove steak from marinade.
3. Remove excess liquid from steak with paper towel.
4. Grill for six minutes on each side.
5. Set aside to rest.
6. Slice pineapple into one-inch disk shape.
7. Grill on high heat for three minutes on each side.
8. Drizzle with reduced balsamic sauce.

FALL RECIPIES

Power Protein Salad
Serves Four

Scrumptious Tips:
This refreshing dish is a great pre and post workout meal that gives you a boost of energy. Mix it up with different seasonal berries and root vegetables that you find at your local farmers markets to make it different each time you prepare it. Try using red and golden beets for great color. I love to use the strawberry balsamic vinegar and lemon infused olive oil from the Olive Oil Store. You can order these from their website (http://sunoliveoil.com/) if there is not a store nearby.

Ingredients:
1 large bag baby organic spinach greens
1 bag organic baby cut carrots
1 bunch beets
1 bag parsnips
1 bag Brussels sprouts, bottom removed, sliced in half lengthwise
1 pint blueberries, blackberries or strawberries (remove stem and slice if using strawberries)
1 can organic garbanzo beans, drained and rinsed
1 bag steamed, shelled edamame
1 small log fresh goat cheese

Directions:
1. Preheat oven to 450° F.
2. Line baking sheet with nonstick foil.
3. Rinse and dry with paper towel (leaving skin on) and chop vegetables.
4. Add 1 tsp olive oil, 1/4 tsp sea salt and 1/4 tsp black pepper, then toss.
5. Spread on baking sheet evenly.
6. Bake for 34 minutes, then broil for one minute on high.
7. Allow to cool for 15 minutes.
8. Combine all ingredients, drizzle with strawberry balsamic vinegar and lemon olive oil, and top with crumbled goat cheese.

Crunchy Kale Salad
Serves Four

Scrumptious Tips:
Kale is a superfood with lots of vitamins, minerals and iron. There are many varieties of kale such as curly, dinosaur and black. Each one has a distinct flavor. I especially love the combination of nuttiness, tartness and bitterness. Always cut out the center rib before chopping the kale, as the rib has a hard, woody texture. Be sure to use a good quality extra virgin olive oil. My favorite for this dish is Arbequena from the Olive Oil Store.

Ingredients:
1 large bunch kale, ribs removed, chopped
1 lemon juiced and zested
1/3 cup roasted and salted pumpkin seeds
1/3 cup shredded parmesan reggiano cheese
1/3 cup extra virgin olive oil

Directions:
Combine all ingredients until well blended.

Quinoa, Corn and Black Bean Salad
Serves Six

Scrumptious Tips:
There are different varieties of quinoa such as tri-colored, traditional, red and black. My favorite is the tri-colored because it is brightly colored and flavorful. Quinoa is a starchy seed that is high in protein, fiber, amino acids, nutrients and minerals. These seeds may look small, but they double in size once they are cooked. Quinoa dishes like this are perfect for make-ahead meals; the flavors enhance when left in the refrigerator overnight and taste delicious served cold or hot.

Ingredients:
1 cup tri-colored quinoa
2 cups vegetable broth
1 can reduced sodium black beans, drained and rinsed
10 ears corn, removed from cob, or one small bag frozen white corn
1 bunch green onions, top and tail removed, thinly sliced
1 package grape tomatoes, cut in half lengthwise
2 fresh banana peppers, stem, seeds and pith removed
1 bunch cilantro, stems removed, finely chopped
6 limes, juiced
1/4 cup extra virgin olive oil
1 tsp salt
1/2 tsp ground cumin
1/2 tsp ground chili
1/2 tsp coriander

Directions:
1. Cook quinoa according to package directions, replacing water with vegetable broth, and set aside.
2. Add remaining items to food processor and finely chop.
3. Stir together quinoa and vegetable mixture until evenly distributed.
4. Serve cold.

Italian Salad
Serves Four

Scrumptious Tips:
Light and flavorful pomegranate balsamic vinegar is what sets this version apart from traditional Italian salads. Pomegranates are rich in vitamin C and immune-building antioxidants and are considered a "super fruit." Make this salad even more colorful and flavor diverse by adding green olives and yellow grape tomatoes. This light dish can be enjoyed for lunch or dinner.

Salad Ingredients:
1 head romaine lettuce, chopped
1 bag shredded carrots
1 red pepper, chopped
1 hot house cucumber, chopped
1 pint organic cherry tomatoes
1 jar pitted Kalamata olives, drained and rinsed

Vinaigrette Ingredients:
1 garlic clove
Dash of sea salt and black pepper
1 tbsp local honey
1 bunch fresh basil
1 bunch fresh curly parsley
1/2 tsp dried oregano
1/3 cup pomegranate vinegar
1 cup extra virgin olive oil

Directions:
1. Assemble salad ingredients together.
2. Blend all items for vinaigrette in food processor until emulsified.
3. Toss vinaigrette into salad.

Festive Apple Salad
Serves Four

Scrumptious Tips:
This dish is a sweet mixture made with apples and nuts. Try different types of apples such as gala, granny smith and cameo for flavor and texture variations. You can substitute honey for maple syrup and lemon rind for orange rind for different flavors. For a more paste-like consistency, add additional nuts and put in a food processor on a high setting for a longer period of time. Spread on top of a cracker with a small amount of red or white horseradish paste for a sweet and spicy flavor.

Ingredients:
2 red apples, chopped
2 green apples, chopped
1/2 cup pecans, chopped
1 tsp ground cinnamon
2 lemons, zested and juiced

Directions:
1. Peel apples and cut into quarters, removing core. Put into food processor on pulse setting until shredded.
2. Add additional ingredients until it reaches a paste-like consistency.

Charred Corn Salad
Serves Four

Scrumptious Tips:

Cut each piece of corn from the cob or use frozen corn. Be sure to use organic and non-GMO. I prefer white corn because it is naturally sweeter. This dish can be served with lunch or dinner—as a side dish or main dish—or on top of salad greens.

Ingredients:

8 cobs white corn, removed from cob, or one small bag frozen white corn
1/2 red onion, minced
1 pint grape tomatoes, halved lengthwise
3 limes, juiced
1 tsp extra virgin olive oil
1 bunch cilantro
1/4 tsp sea salt
1/4 tsp black pepper
1/2 jalapeño, seeds and pith removed, minced
1 can organic black beans, drained and rinsed

Directions:

1. In skillet, sauté onion and jalapeño in oil on medium-high heat for two minutes.
2. Add corn to sauté pan and cook for additional three minutes.
3. In large bowl, mix together additional ingredients.

Tropical Coconut Fruit Salad
Serves Four

Scrumptious Tips:
This dish is packed full of delicious fruits and nuts, with the addition of shredded coconut. Coconut is high in fiber and its naturally sweet flavor complements the various fruits. The texture also pairs nicely with the crunch of the almonds.

Ingredients:
4 red apples
1 and 1/2 cups halved green grapes
2 oranges
1 large can pineapple chunks
1/2 large pomegranate
1/2 cup shredded unsweetened coconut
1/4 cup sliced almonds
1/2 cup grape juice (or more, to taste)
1/2 lemon, juiced

Directions:
1. Dice apples and oranges, cut green grapes in half, and mix in pomegranate seeds.
2. Add lemon juice, coconut and almonds, followed by grape juice. Mix and serve in small bowls.

Pulled Chicken Avocado Salad
Serves Six

Scrumptious Tips:

It's essential to poach the chicken for pulled chicken salad. Using the low temperature and moist heat cooking method described in the directions cooks the chicken gently, prevents it from overcooking and ensures it's tender. Serve inside of a sandwich or on top of your favorite greens.

Ingredients:

4 organic chicken breasts (two pounds), poached, shredded
4 limes, juiced and zested
1 bunch green onions, thinly sliced
1 bunch cilantro, finely chopped
1/4 tsp jalapeño pepper, pith and seeds removed, diced
1 Florida avocado, peeled, pitted and diced
1/4 tsp ground chipotle powder to taste
Sea salt and black pepper to taste
3 tbsps organic Vegenaise®

Directions:

1. In large pot, cover chicken with water.
2. Bring water to boil, turn down heat to low, cover and cook for 20 minutes or until no longer pink and center of meat reaches 165° F.
3. Shred chicken.
4. Stir together all ingredients until well combined.

Vegetable Minestrone Soup
Serves Six

Scrumptious Tips:
Using fresh herbs adds a burst of flavor to this soup. If kidney beans are not your favorite, you can substitute any kind of bean that you prefer. This soup improves in time as it sits overnight in the refrigerator, but remember to be conservative with the salt because the salt comes out more as it sits. Make a large vat and keep some in the refrigerator for a few days. It's also great to freeze. To defrost, remove from the freezer and place in the refrigerator overnight.

Ingredients:
1 tbsp olive oil
1 Vidalia onion, chopped
3 stalks chopped celery
2 cloves garlic, minced
1 bag chopped organic carrots
8 cups organic vegetable broth
1 can organic garbanzo beans, rinsed and drained
1 can organic dark red kidney beans, rinsed and drained
1 28 oz can organic diced tomatoes
1 zucchini, chopped
1 squash, chopped
1 bag fresh organic baby spinach
1 bag French style green beans, chopped
1 bag fresh basil, stems removed, chopped
6 sprigs fresh oregano, stems removed, chopped
1/2 tsp sea salt
1 tsp of black pepper

Directions:
1. Sauté onion, celery and garlic in olive oil over medium-high heat for two minutes.
2. Combine additional ingredients, turn heat to high, bring to boil, turn down to medium-low heat and cover.
3. Simmer over medium-low heat for 30 minutes.

Roasted OLD BAY® Steak Fries with Dipping Sauce
Serves Four

Scrumptious Tips:
OLD BAY® is a Maryland favorite, and it has a great balance of salty and spicy flavors that go with most foods. These hand cut, seasoned steak fries are easy to make and sure to please everyone in the family, making them a perfect side dish, snack or party food!

Steak Fries Ingredients:
4 baking potatoes, cut into wedges
1/2 tsp OLD BAY® Seasoning
1/8 cup extra virgin olive oil

Dipping Sauce Ingredients:
1 tbsp Vegenaise®
1/4 cup ketchup
1/4 tsp hot sauce

Steak Fries Directions:
1. Preheat oven to 450° F.
2. Line baking sheet with nonstick foil.
3. Line potatoes in single layer and roast in center rack of oven for 35 minutes.

Dipping Sauce Directions:
1. Toss ingredients together in large bowl.
2. Whisk together all ingredients to serve with fries.

Maryland Style Chicken Salad
Serves Four

Scrumptious Tips:
OLD BAY® puts a nice twist on traditional chicken salad. Using a plain rotisserie chicken lends a nice contrast of both white and dark meat, giving this salad a delicate texture and flavor.

Ingredients:
1 rotisserie chicken, pulled
1⁄4 cup Original Vegenaise®
1 lemon, juiced
1 tsp OLD BAY® Seasoning
3 stalks celery, minced
1⁄2 sweet onion, minced

Directions:
1. Combine all ingredients in food processor and pulse until well blended.
2. Serve on top of greens.

Baked Egg Rolls with Dipping Sauce
Serves Six

Scrumptious Tips:
These light and delicious egg rolls are a healthy and tasty alternative to traditional deep fried egg rolls. The tangy, homemade dipping sauce adds a nice kick! If you are not a fan of seafood, you can substitute for ground pork or chicken. Various varieties of soy sauce and soy sauce alternatives are available to suit your dietary preferences, such as gluten-free, reduced sodium, coconut aminos and Bragg Liquid Aminos.

Egg Rolls Ingredients:
1 package egg roll wrappers (produce section)
1 cup baby shrimp, cooked
1 lb cooked ground organic lean pork or chicken
1 bunch scallions, thinly sliced
1/2 package shredded carrots
1/4 cup gluten-free reduced sodium soy sauce, coconut aminos or Bragg Liquid Aminos
1/4 tsp crushed red peppers

Dipping Sauce Ingredients:
1/4 cup gluten-free, reduced sodium soy sauce, coconut aminos or Bragg Liquid Aminos
1/2 tsp ginger paste
1/2 tsp garlic paste
2 dots of Sriracha chili sauce
1 tsp local honey

Egg Rolls Directions:
1. Combine all ingredients and stir together until combined.
2. Scoop 1/4 cup mixture into egg roll.
3. Wrap according to directions on package.
4. Line baking sheet with nonstick foil.
5. Bake seam side down at 375° F for 15 minutes.

Dipping Sauce Directions:
Whisk ingredients together and serve with egg rolls.

Apple Cranberry Sauce
Serves Six

Scrumptious Tips:
This versatile and deliciously sweet and tangy sauce can be used to complement many breakfast, lunch or dinner recipes. Using sweet red variety of apples such as pink lady or gala will lend a more robust flavor. Try topping your favorite pancake or waffle recipe, grilled or roasted chicken, pork chops or roasted vegetables, use it as a sweet and tangy spread on a sandwich or a dipping sauce for a creative egg roll. The list of options could go on and on!

Ingredients:
4 apples, peeled, cored and chopped
1/2 bag fresh cranberries
1 lemon, juiced
1 tsp cinnamon
1 tsp honey
2 cups water

Directions:
1. Place all ingredients in pot, bring to boil, turn heat to low and cover.
2. Simmer for 20 minutes.
3. Mash mixture together.

Smoky Pepper and Charred Corn Medley
Serves Four

Scrumptious Tips:

I love white corn for its sweet flavor and crisp texture, and prefer either local organic corn from the farmers market or frozen certified non-GMO organic corn. To prepare fresh shucked corn, rinse in a colander under cold water to remove any remaining silk, and pat dry with a paper towel.

Ingredients:

1 tbsp organic olive oil
8 stalks of white corn or one large bag organic non-GMO certified frozen white corn
1 red onion, finely chopped
3 garlic cloves, minced
1 poblano pepper, seeds and pith removed
Pinch of salt
Pinch of ground chipotle pepper
1 lime, juiced
1 bunch cilantro, finely chopped

Directions:

1. In nonstick pan, sauté all ingredients, excluding lime and cilantro, in olive oil on medium-high heat for five minutes.
2. Remove from the heat, and toss into lime and cilantro.

French Green and Wax Bean Medley with Pancetta
Serves Four

Scrumptious Tips:
French green beans are aesthetically pleasing and have a more delicate taste than other varieties of green beans. Wax beans add a nice color contrast to pair with the green beans. Pancetta is Italian ham, but if you prefer bacon, you can make the substitution. Serve as a side dish or as a main entrée with roasted salmon on top.

Ingredients:
1 small package French green beans
1 small package wax beans
1 package pancetta
1/2 tsp cracked black pepper
1 tsp extra virgin olive oil

Directions:
1. Preheat oven to 375° F.
2. Line half sheet baking pan with nonstick foil.
3. Line pancetta in single layer.
4. Bake on middle rack for 10 minutes or until crispy and slightly browned.
5. While pancetta is in oven, turn a large nonstick pan or skillet on medium-high heat, add olive oil, and sauté beans for three minutes, tossing every minute.
6. Remove pancetta from oven, transfer to plate and cool.
7. Crumble pancetta and toss into beans.

Baby Kale and Red Pepper Medley
Serves Four

Scrumptious Tips:
Kale actually grows tastier leaves after frost, so even though you can get it in July, it's sweeter later in the year. I love to use a mixture of baby kale varieties as the younger leaves have more of a delicate taste and texture. This dish is a great complement to my Smoky Roasted Chicken recipe. Feel free to substitute any of your favorite peppers to make it work for your taste.

Ingredients:
1 tbsp olive oil
1 Vidalia onion, thinly sliced
1 large red bell pepper, cut into thin strips
1/2 red chili pepper, minced
3 cloves garlic, chopped
1/2 tsp salt
1/4 tsp black pepper
1 large bunch organic baby kale

Directions:
1. Sauté onion, red bell pepper, red chili pepper, garlic, salt and pepper in olive oil on medium-high heat for three minutes.
2. Add kale and sauté for additional two minutes.

Sweet Potato Tzimmes
Serves Four

Scrumptious Tips:
This is a versatile dish that can be served as breakfast, lunch, dinner, a side dish or even dessert. For a complete vegan meal, mix in chickpeas. The natural sweetness and caramelization of the vegetables and fruits really comes out in this dish, making it a great complement to any meal.

Ingredients:
1 lb carrots, peeled, cut into one-inch discs, cooked in boiling water for five minutes
6 sweet potatoes, peeled, cut into one-inch discs, cooked in boiling water for five minutes
1/2 orange, juiced
A dash of salt and pepper
1/4 tsp cinnamon
1 cup pitted prune, chopped
1 tsp olive oil

Directions:
1. Preheat oven to 375° F.
2. Mix everything together.
3. Cover with foil.
4. Bake for 30 minutes.
5. Uncover and bake for additional 10 minutes.

Citrusy White Sweet Potato and Black Bean Salad
Serves Four

Scrumptious Tips:
The white colored sweet potatoes are a unique variety of sweet potatoes that have a sweeter flavor and softer texture than their counterparts. Serve this dish cold as a side salad, or on top of your favorite grilled or roasted meat, fish or tofu.

Ingredients:
1 tsp olive oil
2 medium white sweet potatoes, peeled and cut into 1/2 inch cubes
1/4 cup red onion, finely diced
1 habanero pepper, seeds and pith removed, finely minced
1 tsp chili powder
1/2 tsp ground cumin
1/4 tsp ground coriander
1 large clove garlic, mashed to paste
1 tsp orange zest, finely grated
1 orange, juiced
1 lime, juiced
1 15 oz. can black beans, rinsed
1 standard bag dried cherries
1/4 cup fresh cilantro, chopped
Dash of sea salt and black pepper

Directions:
1. Cover potatoes with water, bring to boil, and simmer for 10 minutes. Drain water and set aside.
2. Mince onions and set aside.
3. Combine and stir together all ingredients.

Roasted Sweet Potatoes with Spices
Serves Four

Scrumptious Tips:

I love to have sweet potatoes year round, but this savory recipe is especially warming and satisfying on crisp autumn days. It also deliciously complements my Smoky Roasted Chicken recipe. Cutting the potatoes into one-inch cubes creates a nice, consistent roasted texture throughout. And by broiling for the last minute, you eliminate the need for stirring or flipping.

Ingredients:

2 lbs sweet potatoes, peeled and cut into one-inch cubes
1 tbsp olive oil
1/4 tsp garlic salt
1/4 tsp black pepper
Dash of sea salt
1 tsp chili powder
1 tsp cinnamon
1 one-inch piece of fresh ginger, peeled and grated
2 limes, juiced
1 tbsp local honey
1 package fresh chives, finely chopped

Directions:

1. Preheat oven to 450° F.
2. Line baking sheet with nonstick foil and spray with oil.
3. In large bowl, combine all ingredients, excluding chives, and toss together until evenly coated.
4. Spread sweet potatoes in single layer on baking sheet.
5. Roast for 34 minutes in middle rack of the oven, then broil for one minute.
6. Remove from oven and sprinkle with chives.

Salmon Cakes with Tartar Sauce
Serves Four

Scrumptious Tips:
Fresh poached salmon has better flavor and texture than canned salmon. Knowing where your fish came from and how it was prepared is an added bonus. If you prefer white fish, you can use cod, flounder or sole.

Salmon Cakes Ingredients:
2 lb fresh salmon, skin removed
2 tbsp fresh parsley, chopped
1 tbsp OLD BAY® Seasoning
1 tbsp sweet onion, diced
1⁄4 cup Original Vegenaise®
1 lemon, juiced
1⁄4 cup panko or gluten-free bread crumbs

Tartar Sauce Ingredients:
1/2 cup Original Vegenaise®
1 tsp. OLD BAY® Seasoning
1 lemon, juiced

Salmon Cakes Directions:
1. Place salmon in water in skillet, bring to boil, then cover and simmer over low heat for 20 minutes.
2. Allow to cool, then flake with fork.
3. Form four small patties and flatten with palm of hand.
4. Arrange patties on prepared baking sheet and broil for four minutes on each side.
5. Serve with lemon wedge.

Tartar Sauce Directions:
1. In small bowl, whisk together all ingredients.
2. Serve cold.

Smoky Roasted Chicken
Serves Four

Scrumptious Tips:
Choose organic and support local farmers if it's an option. Dry the chicken with a paper towel so that it browns without steaming. The bone-in chicken is great for reheating because it's moist and does not dry. If you buy from the grocery or butcher, ask them to remove the skin to save you time. When removing the chicken from the oven, set it aside to rest for 1/3 of the cooking time so the juices seal.

Ingredients:
4 bone-in chicken leg and thigh quarters, skin removed
2 lemons, juiced
2 tsp sea salt
1/2 tsp hot smoked Spanish paprika
1/2 tsp ground chipotle powder
2 tsp extra virgin olive oil
1 head garlic, skin removed

Directions:
1. Preheat oven to 375° F.
2. Line baking sheet with nonstick foil and spray with oil.
3. Dry chicken with paper towel.
4. Spread garlic on baking sheet before placing chicken on top, in single layer.
5. Pour lemon juice on top of chicken.
6. In small bowl, mix together seasoning and olive oil and cover chicken with even coat.
7. Roast for 44 minutes, uncovered in middle rack of oven.
8. Move baking sheet to top rack and broil on high heat for one minute.
9. Let chicken rest for 10 minutes.

Sun-dried Tomato, Broccoli and Chicken Pasta
Serves Four

Scrumptious Tips:

Bursting with the robust flavors of sun-dried tomatoes, fresh thyme and parmesan cheese, this hearty pasta dish is perfectly satisfying on a crisp autumn evening. Marinate the chicken for a minimum of 30 minutes, but 6-8 hours for best results.

Ingredients:

1 lb chicken tenderloins
1 lemon, juiced
1 tbsp Worcestershire sauce
Dash of garlic salt and black pepper
1 lb cooked whole wheat or gluten-free rotini pasta
1/2 jar sun-dried tomatoes with herbs
1 tsp extra virgin olive oil
12 oz chopped broccoli
1/4 cup freshly grated parmesan cheese
6 sprigs thyme, removed from stem

Directions:

1. Marinate chicken in Worcestershire sauce.
2. Squeeze lemon on top of chicken.
3. Season with salt and pepper.
4. Grill on high heat for four minutes on each side.
5. Set chicken aside on cutting board.
6. Toss remaining ingredients in pasta.
7. Chop chicken and add to pasta.

Middle Eastern Spiced Chicken
Serves Eight

Scrumptious Tips:

I love to add sumac powder to Middle Eastern style dishes. It has a citrusy, tart flavor and is a deep purplish color. Za'atar is a spice blend with sesame seeds, sumac and thyme. You can find these spices in stores or online at penzeys.com. Instead of chicken, this dish can be prepared with super firm tofu, tempeh or your favorite seafood. It also goes well with all vegetables!

Ingredients:

1/2 tsp sumac powder
1/2 tsp Za'atar seasoning
1/2 tbsp cumin
1/2 tbsp paprika
1/2 tsp coriander
1/2 tsp oregano
1/2 tsp crushed red pepper flakes
1/2 tsp sea salt
8 boneless, skinless chicken cutlets
1/4 cup extra virgin olive oil
1 lemon, juiced

Directions:

1. Combine spices.
2. Tenderize chicken cutlets using tenderizing mallet.
3. Add spices, olive oil and lemon to chicken.
4. Set chicken aside and marinate for at least 15 minutes.
5. Grill chicken for five minutes on each side or until it reaches an internal temperature of 165° F.
6. Slice chicken by cutting across the grain.

Herb Roasted Turkey Breast
Serves Four

Scrumptious Tips:
Using all natural bone-in turkey breasts lends to a more succulent dish when cooked and reheated. Make a couple on the weekend to slice up and use hot or cold in various dishes throughout the week.

Ingredients:
1 bone-in turkey breast (3-4 lbs)
1⁄4 cup Worcestershire sauce
Salt and pepper to taste
4 garlic cloves, skin removed, minced
1 lemon, zested and juiced
1⁄4 cup olive oil
1 package fresh herb blend (thyme, rosemary, sage) removed from stems and finely chopped

Directions:
1. Sprinkle turkey with Worcestershire sauce, salt and pepper.
2. Put remaining ingredients into food processor until it forms a smooth mixture.
3. Rub mixture on top of turkey.
4. Bake at 375° F for 1.5 hours or until a thermometer placed in the thickest part of the turkey reaches 165° F.
5. Remove from oven, allow meat to rest for about 1/3 of its total cooking time, and pull from bone.

WINTER RECIPIES

Honey Nut Chex Mix
Serves 12

Scrumptious Tips:

This gluten-free snack is a delicious nutty and fruity mix with an excellent balance of salty and sweet. Honey Nut Chex mix is a special treat for people of all ages to enjoy! Put it in individual baggies or containers for an easy snack on the go.

Ingredients:

1 12 oz box Honey Nut Chex cereal
1/2 tsp cinnamon
1 16 oz container salted, roasted cashews
2 bags dried cherries
1 bag semi-sweet dark chocolate mini morsels

Directions:

1. Preheat oven to 375° F.
2. Mix together cinnamon and Chex cereal.
3. Bake for 12 minutes, stirring every four minutes.
4. Cool and add additional ingredients.
5. Store at room temperature in airtight container or in baggies to retain freshness.

Roasted Red Pepper Hummus
Serves Eight

Scrumptious Tips:
Hummus is a traditional Middle Eastern "puréed salad" made from cooked chickpeas and tahini, which is a ground sesame seed paste. It can be eaten as an appetizer, dip, spread or sandwich filling inside falafel. Hummus complements raw vegetables, pita chips, pita bread, flatbread and crackers. It can be made with a variety of flavors such as roasted red pepper, lemon and garlic.

Ingredients:
2 cans organic chickpeas, drained and rinsed
2 tbsp tahini paste
1 jar roasted red peppers, drained and rinsed
1/4 cup extra virgin olive oil
Dash of sea salt, black pepper, ground cayenne pepper and paprika

Directions:
1. Place all ingredients, excluding paprika, in food processor.
2. Turn on high speed and slowly add water until it reaches a smooth consistency.
3. Place in bowl and garnish with paprika.

Sun-dried Tomato and Herb Goat Cheese Spread with Toast Points
Serves Six

Scrumptious Tips:
This crowd-pleasing goat cheese spread is full of robust flavors from fresh herbs and sweet sun-dried tomatoes, making it the perfect dish for potluck parties. Be sure to use fresh herbs and support your local goat cheese maker by purchasing from local vendors whenever possible. Fresh is always best!

Ingredients:
2 tbsp flat-leaf parsley leaves, finely chopped
2 tbsp thyme leaves, removed from stem
1 16 oz goat cheese log
1 cup sun-dried julienne tomatoes in oil
1 package basil, thinly sliced

Directions:
1. Combine first three ingredients until well blended.
2. Spread one teaspoon of goat cheese spread onto each toast point.
3. Top with 1/2 teaspoon of sun-dried tomatoes and pinch of basil leaves.

Mediterranean Fruit Salad
Serves Four

Scrumptious Tips:
Try a different blend of dried fruits to fit your preference, such as apricots, cherries, cranberries, dates and figs. Various nuts that would go nicely are almonds, walnuts and cashews. Purchase dried fruits and nuts that are all natural, low-sodium and use olive oils, with no added sugars.

Ingredients:
8 oranges, peeled and chopped
5 pitted figs, chopped
4 bananas, chopped
1 cup golden raisins
1 cup walnuts, chopped
1/4 cup grape juice

Directions:
Combine and stir ingredients together until well incorporated.

Roasted Coconut Butternut Squash Soup
Serves Six

Scrumptious Tips:
Butternut squash is a winter squash that has a sweet, nutty taste. When it's ripe, it turns a dark orange color. It can be roasted, puréed or mashed. Remove the top and tail end, cut in half lengthwise, scoop out the seeds, peel the skin and chop. It's very filling and satisfying!

Ingredients:
2 leeks, white part, rinsed and chopped
1 large butternut squash cut in half lengthwise, seeds removed and chopped, or 1 bag frozen butternut squash chopped
4 cups organic vegetable broth
1/2 tsp ground cayenne pepper
1 can organic coconut milk
2 tbsp fresh rosemary, chopped

Directions:
1. Preheat oven to 400° F.
2. Line baking sheet with nonstick foil and spread squash in single layer.
3. Roast for 34 minutes, then broil on high heat for one minute.
4. Sauté garlic and leek in olive oil on medium heat for two minutes.
5. Combine additional ingredients in large pot and bring to boil. Turn down heat to simmer, cook uncovered for 10 minutes, and stir in butternut squash.
6. Run through blender until it reaches a smooth consistency.

Maryland Style Crab Soup
Serves Six

Scrumptious Tips:

When I think of Maryland style cuisine, I think of OLD BAY® Seasoning, with the smoky paprika and celery seed permeating every bite of my favorite crab soup. The natural buttery texture and flavor of honey gold potatoes pairs beautifully with the robust flavors and textures of the fresh, sweet white corn and French-style green beans. Allow the pan to heat up for 30 seconds before adding oil, then allow oil to sit in the pan for 30 more seconds.

Ingredients:

1 piece of onion (If it sizzles, you know the pan is hot enough.)
1 vidalia onion, finely chopped
2 stalks celery, finely chopped
1 tbsp OLD BAY® Seasoning
8 cups organic vegetable broth
1 28 oz can organic diced tomatoes
10 honey gold potatoes, cut in half
3 stalks fresh white corn kernels
1 package fresh French-style green beans, chopped
1 bunch parsley, chopped

Directions:

1. Sauté onion, celery and garlic in olive oil over medium-high heat for two minutes.
2. Combine additional ingredients, excluding crab meat and parsley, turn heat to high, bring to boil, turn down to medium-low heat and cover.
3. Simmer over medium-low heat for 30 minutes, stir in crab and cook an additional five minutes.

Mini Potato Frittatas
Serves 12

Scrumptious Tips:
This high-protein, filling dish is great for breakfast, lunch or dinner! The individually portioned size makes grab-and-go meals easy, and it's perfect for storing in the refrigerator or freezer for later. For a different twist on this dish, try incorporating your favorite shredded cheese or vegetables such as shredded carrots, chopped mushrooms, peppers or kale.

Ingredients:
Nonstick organic pure olive oil spray
1 small bag baby spinach, cooked, moisture squeezed out
1 bag shredded potatoes (found in fresh section of grocery store)
1 package fresh chives, minced
1/4 cup shredded organic sharp cheddar cheese

Directions:
1. Preheat oven to 375° F.
2. Spray each muffin cup with olive oil spray.
3. Whisk ingredients together until well blended.
4. Fill each muffin cup 3/4 of the way to top.
5. Remove from oven, cool, and remove from muffin cups.

Chipotle White Sweet Potatoes
Serves Four

Scrumptious Tips:
White organic sweet potatoes have a sweet taste and creamy texture. The sea salt and smoky flavors balance the flavor of the naturally sweet potatoes, satisfying both your sweet and salty cravings!

Ingredients:
4 white organic sweet potatoes, sliced in 1/2 inch round discs, skin on
1 tsp smoked sea salt or course sea salt
1/4 cup chili-infused olive oil

Directions:
1. Preheat oven to 450° F.
2. Line baking sheet with nonstick foil.
3. In large mixing bowl, toss together potatoes and additional ingredients until evenly coated.
4. Line potatoes on baking sheet in single layer.
5. Bake in center rack of oven for 34 minutes, then broil on low heat for one minute.

Sweet and Spicy Roasted Sweet Potatoes with Honey Butter
Serves Four

Scrumptious Tips:
The cinnamon flavor and sweet potatoes reminds me of the holiday season, and the honey dipping sauce makes this dish great for breakfast, lunch, dinner or even a side item or dessert!

Sweet Potato Ingredients:
4 organic sweet potatoes, sliced into 1/4 inch discs, skin on
1/4 tsp ground cayenne pepper
3 sprigs rosemary, stem removed, finely chopped
1/4 cup organic extra virgin olive oil

Honey Butter Ingredients:
1 tbsp local orange blossom honey
1/4 cup whipped butter or butter alternative

Sweet Potato Directions:
1. Preheat oven to 450° F.
2. Line baking sheet with nonstick foil.
3. Toss sweet potatoes in oil and additional ingredients until evenly coated.
4. Spread sweet potatoes in single layer on baking sheet.
5. Bake in center rack of oven for 40 minutes.

Honey Butter Directions:
Whisk together all ingredients until well blended.

Chunky Vegetable Marinara Sauce
Serves Six

Scrumptious Tips:
I prefer to use local organic produce when it's available. Not only because I like to avoid unnecessary chemicals in my diet, but also because the flavor is usually better than conventionally grown fruits and vegetables. Organic tomatoes have a more robust flavor, and organic carrots always taste sweeter. This recipe can also be puréed in the food processor to give it a smoother texture.

Ingredients:
1⁄4 cup of your favorite red wine
2 large cans organic crushed tomatoes, or 2 lbs fresh tomatoes chopped with seeds removed
2 carrots, peeled and minced
1 bunch fresh parsley, chopped
1⁄4 tsp celery seed
1⁄4 tsp oregano
1⁄4 tsp sea salt
1⁄4 tsp black pepper
1⁄4 tsp crushed red pepper
1 bunch fresh basil, chopped

Directions:
1. Sauté onion and garlic in olive oil on medium-high heat for two minutes.
2. Add red wine, turn heat up to high to bring to boil, and cook for two minutes.
3. Add remaining ingredients except for basil.
4. Cover and reduce heat to simmer for 30 minutes.
5. Garnish with fresh, chopped basil.
6. Serve on top of bed of spaghetti squash, whole wheat penne pasta or gluten-free pasta, and turkey meatballs.

Turkey Meatballs
Serves Six

Scrumptious Tips:
Using ground turkey instead of ground beef makes these meatballs a
low-fat, low-cholesterol and heart-healthy choice. The ricotta cheese
gives them a wonderful fluffy and moist texture. If you are on a gluten-
free diet, substitute gluten-free breadcrumbs for the whole wheat
bread crumbs. If you avoid dairy, substitute an additional egg for the
ricotta cheese. Since turkey meatballs freeze and reheat well, they are a
great dish to make ahead of time and enjoy later.

Ingredients:
Nonstick organic pure olive oil spray
2 lbs 94% fat free, all natural ground turkey
1/2 cup whole wheat Panko bread crumbs
1/2 cup low-fat ricotta cheese
1/4 tsp garlic salt, black pepper and ground red pepper

Directions:
1. Preheat oven to 350° F and line baking sheet with nonstick aluminum
foil.
2. Spray foil with light coating of nonstick spray.
3. Mix all ingredients together, then hand-roll mixture into walnut sized
balls.
4. Serve with your favorite marinara sauce.

Cauliflower Rice
Serves Four

Scrumptious Tips:
This is another low carb dish that is great in place of rice! It makes a terrific side dish to serve alongside your favorite protein and vegetables. Several varieties of cauliflower exist that come in different colors and crossbreeds, such as purple and green. "Broccoliflower" is a cross between broccoli and cauliflower.

Ingredients:
1 tsp unrefined coconut oil
1 cauliflower, leaves and center removed, cut into florets
3 garlic cloves, chopped
Sea salt and black pepper to taste

Directions:
1. In medium sized pot, cover cauliflower with water, bring to boil, cover, and turn to medium heat. Cook for 15 minutes before draining.
2. Add all ingredients to food processor and pulse until it reaches a chunky, mashed potato texture.

Balsamic Rosemary Roasted Vegetable Medley
Serves Eight

Scrumptious Tips:
This makes a great tapas dish paired with wine, a filling and satisfying vegetarian main dish or a side dish. Mix it up by using different combinations of local vegetables each time you prepare it. Use local goat cheese and balsamic vinegar from The Olive Oil store for the best quality and taste.

Ingredients:
1 small bag organic baby carrots, dried with paper towel
1 head cauliflower, core removed, chopped
1 head broccoli, core removed, chopped
4 sprigs rosemary, stem removed, finely chopped
1/4 cup extra virgin olive oil
1 small goat cheese log, crumbled
1/4 cup high quality balsamic vinegar

Directions:
1. Preheat oven to 450° F.
2. Line baking sheet with nonstick foil.
3. Toss ingredients together, excluding goat cheese and vinegar.
4. Line vegetable mixture in single layer on baking sheet.
5. Bake on middle rack of oven for 40 minutes, tossing every 20 minutes.
6. Remove from oven.
7. Top with goat cheese and drizzle with balsamic vinegar.

Leek Stuffing
Serves Six

Scrumptious Tips:
Leeks reach their peak in the winter months, making this a great side dish for the holidays. To make this recipe gluten free, simply substitute gluten-free bread for the loaf of sourdough. To make it vegan, vegetable broth can be substituted for the chicken broth.

Ingredients:
6 leeks, rinsed, green part removed, chopped
1 loaf sourdough bread, cut into cubes
1 cup low-sodium organic chicken broth

Directions:
1. Preheat oven to 375° F.
2. Bake bread cubes for 20 minutes.
3. Stir together remaining ingredients and combine bread cubes.
4. Bake in casserole dish covered with foil for 30 minutes.
5. Remove foil and serve.

Mexican Style Stuffed Peppers
Serves Eight

Scrumptious Tips:
To make these less of a mess to eat, cut the pepper lengthwise, creating an open-faced pepper. A variety of different colored bell peppers can be used; for a spicier version, use poblano peppers. Try to find an organic salsa that has minimal ingredients or use your own homemade version. Brown rice can be used instead of quinoa; for a low carb option, omit the rice or quinoa.

Ingredients:
1 lb white and dark ground chicken blend
1 jar medium organic salsa
1/4 tsp ground chipotle pepper
2 cups cooked brown rice or quinoa
1/2 cup Mexican cheese blend

Directions:
1. With nonstick medium-sized sauté pan, turn to medium heat for one minute, add oil for 30 seconds, add chicken, and sauté for three minutes or until no longer pink.
2. In large bowl, stir together cooked rice, salsa, half of the cheese and chicken.
3. Cut peppers in half lengthwise, remove stems, seeds and pith, boil in water (covering peppers) for 12 minutes or until soft.
4. Remove from water.
5. Stuff each pepper with mixture and sprinkle with remaining cheese.
6. Broil on lined baking sheet for one minute or until cheese is brown and bubbly on top.

Cayenne Glazed Salmon
Serves Four

Scrumptious Tips:
Cayenne gives this glazed salmon recipe a nice color and spicy flavor, but you can also switch it up with smoked paprika, chipotle, chili powder or sumac for a Middle Eastern flavor. Use a fine microplane to zest fresh lemon for an extra zing. Choose a raw, local honey that is unfiltered and unprocessed. Regularly consuming local honey can be helpful for those who suffer with allergies.

Ingredients:
4 pieces of 8 oz salmon, skin on
2 lemons, juiced
1/4 cup local orange blossom honey
Sea salt and black pepper to taste
Dash of cayenne pepper
1 bunch flat leaf parsley, finely chopped

Directions:
1. Preheat oven to 350° F.
2. Line baking sheet with nonstick foil.
3. Spread fish in single layer.
4. Pierce fish with fork.
5. Sprinkle with all ingredients, excluding parsley, and adding honey last.
6. Bake for 14 minutes, then broil for one minute on high heat.
7. Remove skin with spatula.
8. Garnish with parsley.

Miso Ginger Glazed Salmon
Serves Four

Scrumptious Tips:
While wild caught fish is usually preferable, some do not enjoy the stronger flavor. Some brands offer farm raised salmon without added color enhancement through feed, making it a better choice than most other farm raised options. A good way to achieve nice color is to add paprika, cayenne, chili, chipotle or any ground pepper. To make the miso, which is fermented soybean paste, peel the outside skin of fresh ginger and use a fine microplane to grate it.

Ingredients:
4 pieces eight oz salmon, skin on
2 limes, juiced
1/8 cup reduced sodium soy sauce
1 inch piece ginger, skin removed, zested
1/2 tsp crushed red pepper seasoning

Directions:
1. Preheat oven to 350° F.
2. Line baking sheet with nonstick foil.
3. Spread fish in single layer.
4. Pierce fish with fork.
5. Sprinkle with all ingredients, adding honey last.
6. Bake for 14 minutes, then broil for one minute on high heat.
7. Remove skin with spatula.

Chipotle Shrimp and Spinach Salad
Serves Four

Scrumptious Tips:
Chipotle peppers are aged, ripened, smoke-dried jalapeños, which are high in heat! The adobe sauce contains vinegar, onions and spices. I love the combination of spicy and sweet in salad dressings. The dressing, charred vegetables, cheese and pumpkin seeds make for a diverse, flavorful salad.

Ingredients:
4 limes, juice and zested
1/3 cup plain rice vinegar
1 cup extra virgin olive oil
2 chilies from one can of adobe chilies
1 tbsp unfiltered and unprocessed local honey
1 bunch cilantro, rinsed and stems removed
1 scallion, rinsed, top and bottom removed
1 lb fresh jumbo shrimp, peeled and deveined
1 bag organic baby spinach
1 small bag frozen white corn
6 sweet baby orange peppers, thinly sliced
1 pint yellow cherry tomatoes, halved
4 oz toasted and salted pumpkin seeds

Directions:
1. Add all dressing ingredients into blender and blend on high until it emulsifies, then set aside.
2. Season shrimp with lime, salt and pepper. Grill on high heat for one minute on each side, then set aside.
3. Sauté corn and peppers on high heat for three minutes until charred.
4. Combine salad ingredients and toss with vinaigrette.

Orange Sesame Roasted Chicken Drumettes
Serves Four

Scrumptious Tips:
You can find black sesame seeds in the ethnic section of the grocery store. I use drumettes because they are easier to eat than large drumsticks, but any cut of bone-in chicken will work. Choose a high quality orange marmalade with the fewest ingredients listed. Peach or apricot preserves are also fantastic alternatives for this recipe!

Ingredients:
12 chicken drumettes (small chicken drumsticks), skin removed
Dash of crushed red pepper flakes
1/4 cup gluten-free soy sauce or soy sauce alternative such as coconut aminos or Bragg Liquid Aminos
4 tbsp high quality orange marmalade
2 tbsp black sesame seeds

Directions:
1. Pierce chicken with fork on both sides.
2. Marinate chicken in soy sauce for 30 minutes.
3. Sprinkle chicken with salt and pepper.
4. Coat chicken with orange marmalade on both sides.
5. Sprinkle with sesame seeds.
6. Roast for 44 minutes, then broil for one minute.

Chicken Stir-Fry
Serves Four

Scrumptious Tips::
I often love to use coconut oil as a healthy alternative cooking oil because the higher smoke point is great for sautéing over high heat, while the oil adds good, healthy fat. If you choose a refined coconut oil, which will usually have a milder flavor and a higher smoke point than unrefined, be sure to avoid the most inexpensive brands, as their refining processes probably are not as healthy. Look for cold pressed refined coconut oil.

Ingredients:
1 lb chicken breast, diced
Dash of sea salt and black pepper to taste
2 tbsp reduced sodium soy sauce
1 cup reduced sodium, organic chicken broth
1 inch peeled fresh ginger, zested
3 garlic cloves, minced
1 bunch scallions, top and tail removed, finely chopped
1/2 tsp red pepper flakes
1 package bean sprouts

Directions:
1. Pierce chicken with fork.
2. Sprinkle chicken with salt and pepper on both sides.
3. Whisk together chicken broth, soy sauce, cornstarch and honey and set aside.
4. Sauté chicken in coconut oil over medium-high heat for five minutes, until no longer pink.
5. Sauté additional vegetables, excluding bean sprouts, on medium-high heat for three minutes.
6. Add broth mixture, turn to high heat, bring to boil, turn down to simmer on medium-low heat, and cook for additional three minutes until sauce has thickened.
7. Top with bean sprouts.

Skirt Steak Chimichurri
Serves Four

Scrumptious Tips::
For a tender skirt steak, use the outside cut, as it requires less marinating time than the inside cut. This dish can also be prepared with grilled chicken, seafood, tofu and even vegetables.

Ingredients:
2 lbs outside organic skirt steak
1 tbsp Worcestershire sauce
1 two oz package fresh oregano, rinsed, stems removed
1 bunch fresh Italian parsley, rinsed, stems removed
1/2 tsp crushed red peppers
3/4 cup organic red wine vinegar

Directions:
1. Marinate steak in Worcestershire sauce for at least 15 minutes.
2. Grill on high heat for five minutes, on each side, or to your desired temperature.
3. Allow meat to rest for five minutes.
4. Thinly slice meat across the grain.
5. In food processor or blender, blend together remaining ingredients on high setting until it reaches a smooth consistency.
6. Combine chimichurri sauce and steak until well blended.

Smoky Burrito Bowl
Serves Four

Scrumptious Tips:
Whether you are a vegetarian or not, this versatile dish can accommodate just about anyone's preferences. My favorite proteins to use for this dish are ground vegetarian crumbles, lean ground beef, or ground white and dark meat chicken blend.

Ingredients:
1 lb ground vegetable crumble, lean ground beef or ground chicken
1 oz packet gluten-free taco seasoning
1/2 tsp ground chipotle powder
2 limes, juiced
1 pineapple, skinned, cored and roughly chopped
1 papaya, peeled and roughly chopped
1 mango, peeled and roughly chopped
1 jalapeño, seeds and pith removed, roughly chopped
1 bunch cilantro, stems removed and roughly chopped
1 head romaine lettuce, chopped

Directions:
1. Sauté protein crumbles in olive oil until no longer pink on medium-high heat for three minutes.
2. Add corn and peppers and sauté for two minutes, or until charred.
3. Add 1/4 cup water, chipotle powder and seasoning and simmer on low-medium heat uncovered for five minutes.
4. Add pineapple, papaya, mango, onion, cilantro, limes and jalapeño to food processor and pulse until chopped and well combined.
5. Layer meat and vegetables, with fruit salsa and lettuce on top.

Whipped Honey-Orange Sweet Potatoes
Serves Four

Scrumptious Tips:
You can achieve a smooth texture and consistency by using a blender, food processor or electric mixer. Feel free to select traditional sweet potatoes, white sweet potatoes, yams or even Japanese sweet potatoes. They range from sweet and mild to a more potent flavor. For a different twist, use butternut squash instead.

Ingredients:
2 large or four small sweet potatoes
1 tsp local honey
Dash of sea salt and pepper
1/4 cup almond milk or milk
1 tbsp whipped butter or dairy free butter
1 orange, juiced

Directions:
1. Peel and chop potatoes, place in large pot, cover with water, and bring to boil. Reduce heat to medium-high, cover, and cook for additional 20 minutes.
2. Using a colander, drain water.
3. Place potatoes and additional ingredients in blender, and pulse until it reaches a smooth texture.

51786865R00058

Made in the USA
Columbia, SC
23 February 2019